Drawing
Thoroughbreds
and Other
Elegant Horses

by Rae Young

CAPSTONE PRESS
a capstone imprint

Snap Books are published by Capstone Press,
1710 Roe Crest Drive, North Mankato, Minnesota 56003
www.capstonepub.com

Library of Congress Cataloging-in-Publication Data
Young, Rae.
  Drawing thoroughbreds and other elegant horses / by Rae Young.
      pages cm. — (Snap. Drawing horses)
  Summary: "Lively text and step-by-step instructions give an introduction to drawing
horses"—Provided by publisher.
  ISBN 978-1-4765-3993-5 (library binding)
  ISBN 978-1-4765-6047-2 (eBook PDF)
1. Horses in art--Juvenile literature. 2. Thoroughbred horse—Juvenile literature.
3. Drawing—Technique—Juvenile literature. I. Title.

  NC783.8.H65Y682 2014e
  743.6'96655—dc23   2013035799

Editorial Credits
Mari Bolte, editor; Lori Bye, designer; Jennifer Walker, production specialist

Photo Credits
All illustrations are by Q2AMedia Services Private Ltd, except for June Brigman, 30-31

Printed in China by Nordica.
1013/CA21301921
092013   007745NORDS14

TABLE OF CONTENTS

GETTING STARTED

Some artists see the world as their canvas. Others see the world as their pasture! If you're a horse lover, grab a pencil and a notebook. Just pick a project and follow the step-by-step instructions. Even if you've never drawn a horse before, the projects in this book will get you started. You'll have everything you need to draw a funny foal or a record-setting racehorse.

Once you've mastered the basics, try giving your art a personal touch. Customize each horse's saddle pad or halter with bright colors and patterns. Add in details like silver conchos or textured leather. Draw accessories such as winter blankets, first-place ribbons, or buckets and brushes. Why not try drawing your friends on a trail ride or galloping across a beach? Don't be afraid to get creative!

TOOLS OF THE TRADE

1. Every artist needs something to draw on. Clean white paper is perfect for creating art. Use a drawing pad or a folder to organize your artwork.

2. Pencils are great for both simple sketches and difficult drawings. Always have one handy!

3. Finish your drawing with color! Colored pencils, markers, or even paints give your equine art detail and realism.

4. Want to add more finishing touches? Try outlining and shading your drawings with artist pens.

5. Don't be afraid of digital art! There are lots of free or inexpensive drawing apps for tablets or smartphones. Apps are a great way to experiment with different tools while on the go.

over fences

Jumping over fences has three main parts—takeoff, flight, and landing. During takeoff, the horse shifts its weight to its back legs. While in flight, the horse stretches it body to clear the fence. During landing, the horse's front legs absorb the impact from its body. Then the horse is ready to canter away to the next fence!

Step 1.

Step 2.

Step 3.

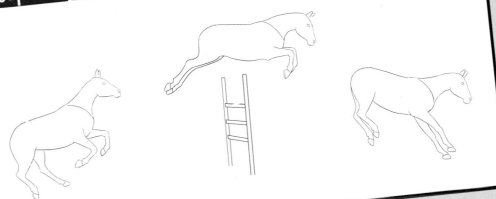

Step 4.

FACT

Add details to your horse to make it a show hunter. Add fancy English tack. Braid its mane and tail. Draw hunter braids as small, thin ovals along the horse's neck.

RIDING ASIDE

Ride like a girl! The first sidesaddle dates from the 1400s. For the next 200 years, ladylike women would ride aside rather than astride. Today riders around the world preserve this ancient style of horsemanship.

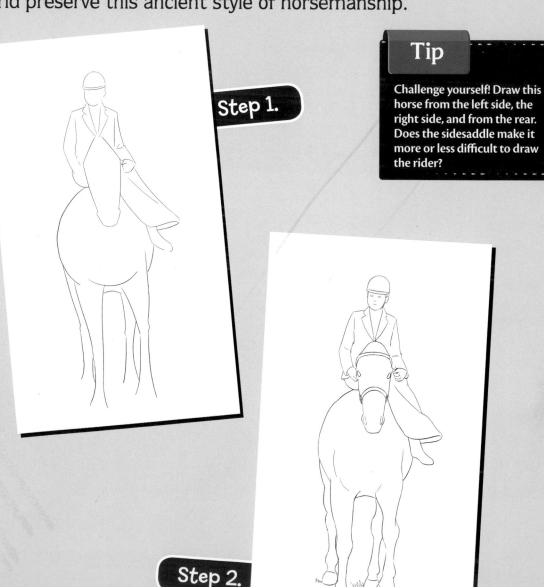

Step 1.

Step 2.

Tip

Challenge yourself! Draw this horse from the left side, the right side, and from the rear. Does the sidesaddle make it more or less difficult to draw the rider?

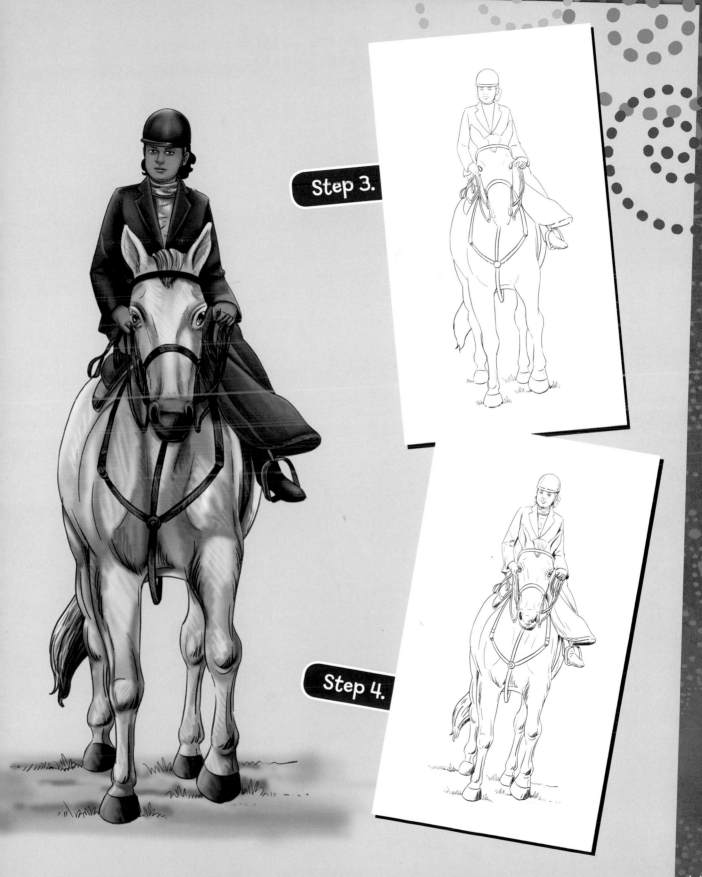

Step 3.

Step 4.

BEACHCOMBER

The Gypsy Vanner was created by European Gypsies. They needed a draft animal in a smaller body. They bred their horses to resemble small, colorful Shires. Today the Gypsy Vanner is recognizable for its bright coat, flowing mane and tail, and thick leg feathering.

Step 1.

Step 2.

Tip

You can color this Gypsy Vanner in any way possible. The most common colors for this breed are black and white (piebald) and brown and white (skewbald).

Step 3.

Step 4.

AIRS ABOVE THE GROUND

Lipizzaners are one of Europe's oldest horse breeds. For more than 440 years, Lipizzaner stallions have been trained to perform the most classical dressage. Their movements are called "airs above the ground." This horse is performing the courbette. The horse balances on its rear legs, then jumps into the air.

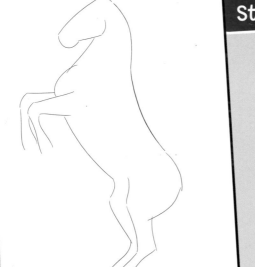

Step 1.

Tip

The Lipizzaner is a Baroque breed. Draw Baroque horses with powerful shoulders and hindquarters, large, arched necks, and thick manes and tails. Other Baroque breeds include the Friesian and Andalusian.

Step 2.

Step 3.

Step 4.

SPEED DUEL

Thoroughbred racehorses can run between
35 and 40 miles (56.3 and 64.4 kilometers)
per hour. Thoroughbreds race distances
of between 5 furlongs, or 660 feet
(200 meters), and 1.5 miles (2.4 km.)

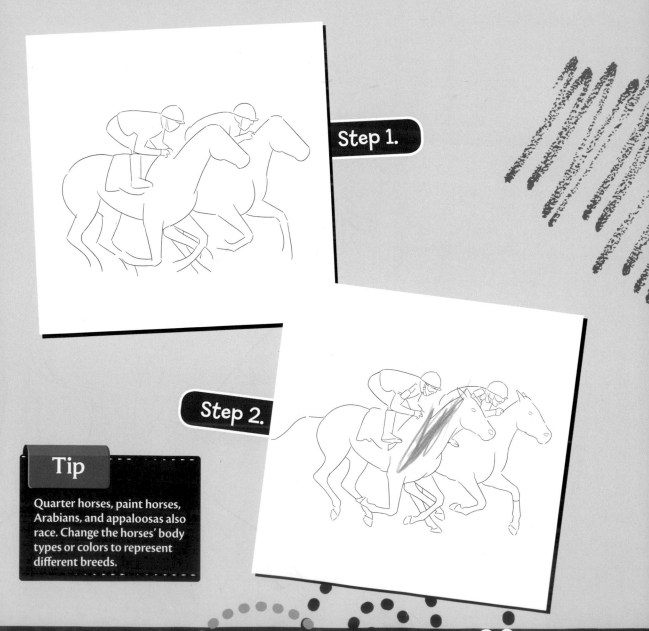

Step 1.

Step 2.

Tip

Quarter horses, paint horses, Arabians, and appaloosas also race. Change the horses' body types or colors to represent different breeds.

Step 3.

Step 4.

CLEAR THE AIR

The Connemara pony is Ireland's only native horse. These ponies are known for kind dispositions and athletic abilities. Don't be afraid to draw big jumps! Connemara ponies have a natural jumping ability, and they often beat larger horses in competitions.

Step 1.

Step 2.

Tip

The most common Connemara pony colors are gray and dun. This pony is fleabitten gray.

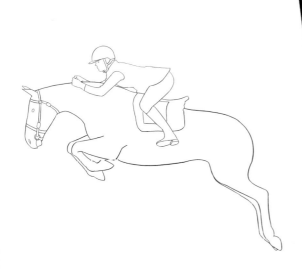

Step 4.

Step 5.

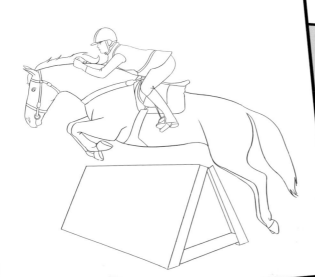

Step 6.

Step 7.

PRETTY MOVER

Peruvian Pasos are gaited horses. Instead of the regular walk, trot, canter, and gallop, their legs move in different patterns. This creates a smoother gait. Draw your horse's tail as still as possible—the less your horse's tail moves, the smoother its gait.

Step 1.

Step 2.

Step 4.

Step 3.

NORWEGIAN FJORD

Like the haflinger, the Norwegian Fjord is a small draft breed. These easily recognizable horses excel under saddle and in harness.

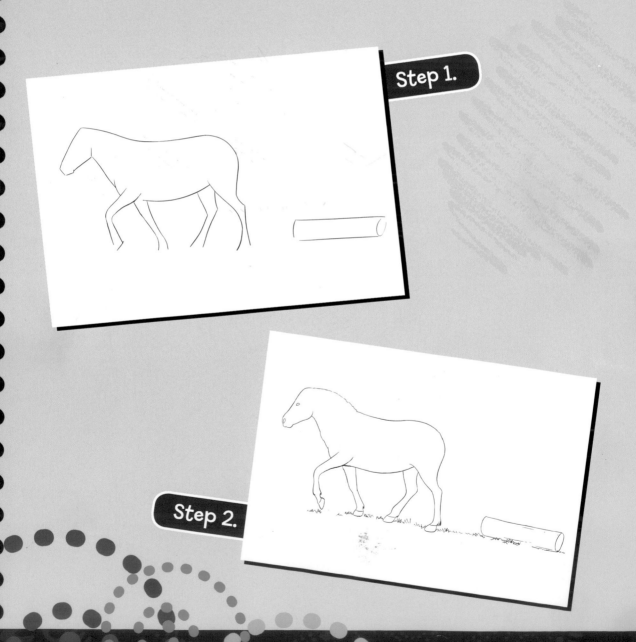

Step 1.

Step 2.

Step 3.

Step 4.

HIGH-LEVEL COMPETITION

Warmbloods are a natural fit for dressage. Their tall bodies and long legs make them ideal for this Olympic sport. Show yours off! During the extended trot, your horse should cover as much ground as possible. Draw it sweeping over the ground with its long, elegant legs stretched out.

Tip

Dressage braids are called button braids. The individual braids are shaped into a ball by using thread or rubber bands. Draw button braids as circles on the horse's neck.

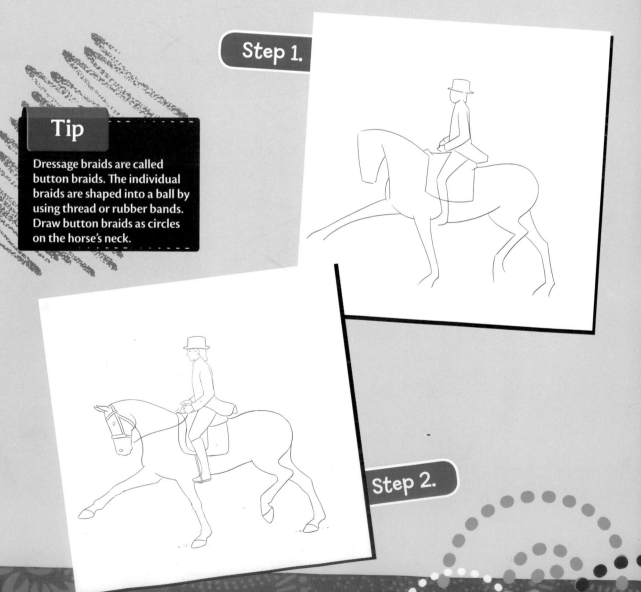

Step 1.

Step 2.

Step 3.

Step 4.

ANOTHER PRETTY FACE

The Arabian's dished head is easily recognizable to most people anywhere. Small, pointed ears and large, expressive eyes give the Arabian its characteristic fire. Draw a long, sweeping mane to help people imagine your horse is galloping across the desert.

Tip

A horse's ears can tell you a lot about what it's feeling. A horse with his ears perked is curious and happy. Ears facing forward or back show the horse is listening. Ears facing outward mean the horse is relaxed and resting. Pinned ears mean pain or anger. Practice showing your horse's emotion by changing the direction its ears face.

Step 1.

Step 2.

Step 3.

Step 4.

FACE FORWARD

Horses have expressive faces. A quick glance should tell you whether the horse is relaxed, awake, or upset. Its eyes, ears, and nose make it clear how it is feeling. This horse is happy and alert.

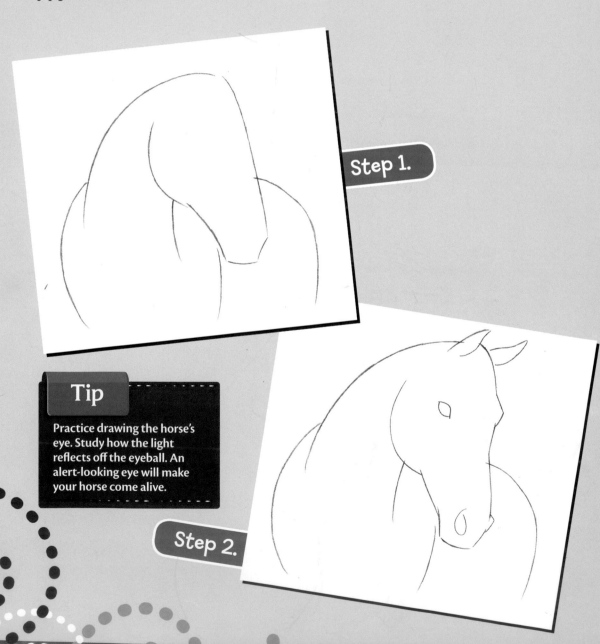

Step 1.

Step 2.

Tip

Practice drawing the horse's eye. Study how the light reflects off the eyeball. An alert-looking eye will make your horse come alive.

Step 3.

Step 4.

INTERNET SITES

FactHound offers a safe, fun way to find Internet sites related to this book. All of the sites on FactHound have been researched by our staff.

Here's all you do:

Visit *www.facthound.com*

Type in this code: 9781476539935

 Check out projects, games and lots more at
www.capstonekids.com

LOOK FOR ALL THE BOOKS IN THIS SERIES

Drawing Appaloosas
and Other Handsome Horses

Drawing Friesians
and Other Beautiful Horses

Drawing Arabians
and Other Amazing Horses

Drawing Mustangs
and Other Wild Horses

Drawing Barrel Racers
and Other Speedy Horses

Drawing Thoroughbreds
and Other Elegant Horses